adult standards  'tidy up' out of existence intelligence and enter ll and already inhibited

This book concerns the child between the age of four and five years, when it develops many new skills, more control over emotions, and closer links with the adult world.

Maybe there are plenty of toys in the home, but do these contribute to your child's development? His toys should be those which are sturdy, simple and adaptable and which encourage both imagination and dexterity.

Complexity is a definite obstruction to imagination. This is why kitchen junk—cartons, plastic bottles, etc.— is so useful. Cartons and bottles will stack and build like bricks; plastic bottles can be cut or shaped for water or sand play or as fitting-together toys—all giving good opportunities for helping your child's development, once you realise the significance of these materials to him. *The subsequent purchase of a really worthwhile toy is then the more easily afforded.*

Although a child in its fifth year shows a great deal of independence, particularly in matters of dressing and washing or when helping Mother, he or she is still very dependent on adults for providing opportunities to practise the skills so rapidly being mastered. Vocabulary is still growing rapidly and is still very dependent on the readiness of grown-ups to talk on all topics likely to interest, educate or amuse.

Your child also needs opportunities to acquire interests outside the home so that development and learning is continuous, and pre-school boredom not allowed to deaden initiative. The bored child becomes the naughty child. The occupied child is a happy child, with fewer behaviour problems and a greater readiness to please. A play-group or nursery school provides these opportunities to acquire outside interests. Failing this, a real effort is necessary on the part of parents to give time and attention. For instance, in most Public Libraries there is a section for the under-fives, to which a child can be taken and where will be found a wide variety of colourful picture 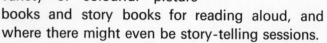 books and story books for reading aloud, and where there might even be story-telling sessions.

This book is intended to help and stimulate all parents who realise the importance of using to the full those situations and materials most likely to develop their child's potential for learning.

Freed

BOOK 4
Four to five years

THE LADYBIRD 'UNDER FIVE' SERIES

Learning
with
Mother

by ETHEL and HARRY WINGFIELD

Publishers: Ladybird Books Ltd . Loughborough
© Ladybird Books Ltd (formerly Wills & Hepworth Ltd) 1971
Printed in England

Joining the library

Most public libraries have a section for the under-fives, displaying a wide variety of colourful picture-books and appealing story books very suitable for reading aloud to this age group.

When joining a library, the young child is introduced to a wider range of books than would otherwise be possible, particularly if parents cannot easily afford books. School at five may be much too late for an effective introduction to books. A good impression is also made on a child who sees the interest and concern with books shown not only by adults but by other children in the library. The Public Library is a happy and interesting introduction to community-provided services (of which primary school will later be a part). Some libraries have story-telling sessions for young children. Enquire at your local library about this.

Taking care of books which are not his own will also help a developing sense of responsibility towards articles and people, and being a member of a library, with his own ticket, will add to his developing sense of social importance.

Talk to your child about the picture, and be a good listener. Say that this part of the library is specially for young children, and that although there is one mother in the picture, children may look at the books by themselves while mothers look at the books for grown-ups in another part of the library. Ask how many children are shown looking at books by themselves. Say that you can spend as much time as you like in a library and that nobody will tell you to hurry. Mention that these children will have to give the librarian their tickets when they leave the library with their books.

0 7214 0275 5

Shapes and puzzles

Simple puzzles and collections of shapes are very good training in quick identification and arrangement, both very necessary when learning words and numbers.

The child in the picture is using coloured cardboard shapes with which he can make both abstract patterns and actual pictures. The card is from cereal packets and Father has marked out the shapes so that they are accurately proportionate to each other; that is, four small squares to make one large one, or four triangles or two oblongs to make the same size square. There are circles, large and small, cut into halves or quarters so that two or four of the same shape and colour fit together. If the card is sufficiently thin it can be cut as well as painted by a child of four.

It is possible to buy puzzles which are graded according to a child's ability. Puzzles of twenty or so pieces are usually suitable for a four-year-old child. The jig-saw illustrated is by Paul and Marjorie Abbatt Ltd.

Care should be taken over choosing puzzles. Any which are too difficult and baffle a child may result in complete loss of interest. The right puzzles must stimulate a feeling of success, even quick success. Children need this kind of gratification as encouragement to further effort.

Talk to your child about the picture and be a good listener. He will probably be happy to learn the words— 'square', 'oblong', 'triangle', 'circle'.

Family outings

Our present way of life tends to restrict a child's activities and his 'learning through experience'. Parents should therefore seek out opportunities for their child to discover more about the world in which he or she lives. What better than a family outing such as boating in the park? This sort of experience, which calls for positive effort from the parents, can do much good because with their help his interests are widened beyond that of the family circle. He also learns many new words.

Because the four-year-old can remember past experiences more easily than a younger child, he will enjoy following up these visits by drawing pictures, or having a scrap book with the word 'Boats' and his own name on the front. In this he can put photographs as well as cut-out pictures. The photographs will help him to recall details he may have forgotten, such as trees round the pool, other boats and the people in them. You can write below his pictures 'John is in a boat' or 'Daddy is rowing'.

He will want to show his book to relatives and friends and talk about the experience to them. To be able to do this gives essential practice in speaking, practice which is of the greatest possible value to the pre-school child.

Talk to your child about the picture, then encourage him to talk about his own experiences. Help him by saying 'When did we do that?' or 'Who was there?' 'Was it a sunny day?' etc.

Boating at home

Here are children playing at 'Boats'—absorbed in repeating an enjoyable experience.

What good is it doing them? They are establishing a deeper understanding of the event; they are using their imagination to think back to the sensations of floating, rocking and gliding over water, or the rather fearful excitement of nearly losing an oar.

All the words new to them when they actually enjoyed the visit to the boating pool they will probably be using in their play, words such as 'rowlock', 'oars', 'stern', 'bow', 'rudder', 'footboard'. They may ask you—'What was this or that thing called?' Help their inventiveness. Join in their world of fantasy with a little conversation and pretence—but not interference. When they start school they may possibly retell their boating experiences to an interested classroom or playground audience.

Whether your child can express himself or herself, can find all the words needed for doing so, depends on the interest and help you have given. Although he will talk to other children, you as an adult are your child's real language teacher long before school age is reached.

Talk about the picture. Encourage your child to talk about 'pretending'. What does he or she like to pretend to be, or pretend to be doing?

Pets Goldfish are fascinating to watch and very little trouble to look after. Having to remember 'Only one pinch of food each day' gives a child a sense of responsibility. He will be interested if the word 'fish' is printed on a label and stuck onto the aquarium. Should your child be unwell and in bed, it will help to dispel boredom if you put the aquarium where the smooth, gliding motion and the glinting colours of the fish can be watched.

One, two, three, four, five,
Once I caught a fish alive,
Six, seven, eight, nine, ten,
Then I let it go again.
Why did you let it go?
Because it bit my finger so.
Which finger did it bite?
This little finger on my right.

Discuss the picture with your child. Does your child know that fish have no eyelids to their eyes? That they can be sleeping as they swim through the water? Remind him that his eyelids close when he is asleep. Tell him that the water which the fish swallows is let out again through its gills. A fish has skin, but skin that is covered with scales. Let him watch you scrape off fish scales next time you prepare fish for cooking.

Ask your child if he thinks that the children take turns to feed the fish. Does he know what is meant by taking turns?

fish

Catching fish   A number of paper 'fish', 'fishing rods' made from pencils or sticks and a length of thread, and 'hooks' consisting of short lengths of 'Sellotape'—these are all you need for this 'fishing competition'.

Draw some fish shapes about six inches long on coloured magazine pages. Try to get realistic shapes— goldfish, mackerel, plaice. Your child can cut them out.

You will find that the 'Sellotape' will readily pick up the fish at a touch. The 'pond' can be a circle of newspaper, or of plastic if you want it to look like water. The winner is obviously the one who catches the most fish.

By three or four years of age, the average child is emotionally able to take the tension of competition with others without developing the tantrums of earlier years. He or she is developing socially and is learning to accept failure as well as to enjoy group play.

Discuss the picture with your child. People have goldfish as pets so that they can watch their movement and beautiful colours. We do not eat goldfish, but there are many fish which we do eat. At the fish shop, point out the different kinds of fish. Tell your child a few of their names, such as plaice or sole which are flat, and mackerel which are long with pretty markings on their backs.

Toys from tyres

Perhaps you, as parents, feel that although the larger, more substantial pieces of play material (swings for instance) are very desirable they also cost more than you can afford.

This need not be so. Much can be done by improvisation. For instance, worn tyres can be had for the asking—so pick a large one. You will need some strong rope to go with it. The rope can be persuaded to stay at opposite sides of the tyre by passing it through holes easily made, for instance, by a hot poker. Another small hole at the bottom of the tyre takes care of rain-water drainage. A good strong support to hang it from, and there's the swing.

Or you can make a bumper truck. Secure the tyre by screws and washers to a substantial wooden platform small enough for the tyre to overhang all round and act as a buffer. Four good castors underneath—or even three, and you have an exciting runabout toy to develop skill and agility in riding, just as the swing encourages agility in climbing, standing to swing, sitting to swing, lying to swing, in all directions—or that thrilling round and round 'twizzle'.

Talk about the picture and be a good listener.

Joining a playgroup

Even the child from the generously-equipped home background will benefit from the stimulating atmosphere of a well run playgroup. He may have already experienced at home many of the activities he finds there, activities such as playing with sand, water, dough, paint, cutting out and sticking together, etc. He may already have had the advantage of playing with another child. The playgroup will offer him all these as well as opportunities for vigorous and adventurous play within an area where supervision is always available.

Books will be there in greater numbers than he may have seen before. To all children there is the challenging step of meeting and accepting the wishes of others. There is also the gratification of having his own efforts acknowledged and praised by other children as well as adults. There is also the joy of moving to music, of singing and listening together. He will develop his powers of self-expression from listening, questioning and answering, and—last but not least—he may experience additional love and affection and so develop emotionally, becoming more mature and ready for an infant school.

Talk about the picture. If your child goes to playgroup or nursery school, let him tell you what he or she does there.

Finger-painting Finding out what can be done with paint, in the way illustrated, is exciting but perhaps more easily done in the playgroup, where larger quantities of paint are available than at home.

The children in the picture have spread powder paint (obtainable from art shops or good toy shops), thickened with Polycel, onto a smooth, washable surface. The girl makes patterns with a comb shape cut from stiff card—more durable shapes can be made from wood. Cotton reels, string, corks, lids, pegs, old tooth brushes and combs all can be used to make interesting patterns, but fingers and palms of hands remain the most natural tools.

Painting in this uninhibited way, using wrist and arm movements, is most beneficial to a child. It can create a feeling of freedom and zest which is likely to be carried over to other occupations and helps the timid child, for example, to become more spontaneous and happy in his play.

If paper is pressed over the paint and carefully lifted off, a print is produced giving the child a permanent record of his effort. Newspaper is suitable—the child itself sees no drawback to its use.

Discuss the picture with your child. Ask what are the colours the children are using. Can he or she also describe the patterns they are making, such as 'curved', 'curly' or 'round and round', 'not straight'. What have they used to make the rings in the red paint?

New shoes

Here is a situation familiar to all children and one full of conversational opportunities. Obviously, too, it is a situation in which they will be expected to behave quietly and politely, since by now they should have sufficient control over their emotions to accept readily this type of minor social discipline.

Should you have to talk to your child about probable behaviour problems, do this beforehand—giving a clear picture of what is expected of him or her. Being admonished in public often results in worse behaviour.

A child's vocabulary at this stage can be very selective and precise. Words for different types of shoe fasteners—'button', 'lace', 'buckle', and words like 'wide', 'narrow', 'tight', 'long', 'short', will all be understood, talked about and enlarged upon afterwards. Encourage your child to acknowledge the help of the assistant.

Ask your child to tell you what is happening and what is shown. Help by suggesting a few words to use, such as 'assistant', 'fitting', or 'measuring'. Point out that the boxes are stacked like bricks.

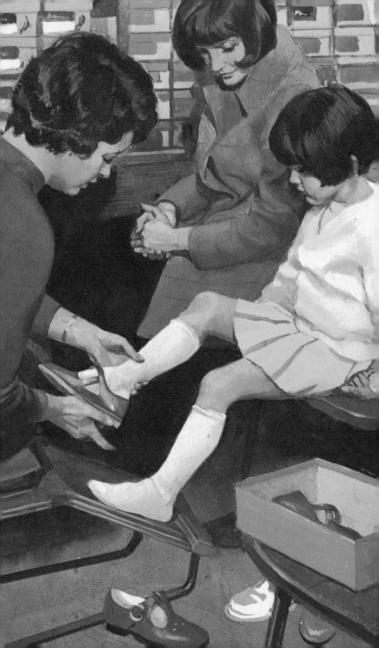

Shoe-box toys

Shoes come in shoe-boxes. And what can be made with a shoe-box? A truck?

Take the box lid and let the child trace four circles on it, drawing round a cup or tin lid. He can then cut out the circles with blunt-nosed scissors, and will then have four wheels. If the card is very firm he may need help, but his own efforts mean the most to him, imperfect though they may be.

Mark the centres for him to make holes with a knitting pin, also the correct places on the box where the wheels will fix. Be sure the wheels will be sufficiently low down. He can now fix on the wheels with brass paper-fasteners, bending over the double ends inside the box.

Or how about a cradle? Mark the box lid across so that one piece is a couple of inches longer than the other. The longer piece makes the headboard—the shorter the footboard. Shape the curves at the bottom of these pieces by drawing round a plate.

Your child can then do the necessary cutting, piercing and fixing with paper-fasteners.

Ask your child to tell you about the picture. Point out details that may not have been observed, such as the two holes in the green lid from where the wheels have been cut.

Hot cross buns

These children are making *real* Hot Cross Buns. Of course they do not go to the oven—Mother will do that. She will also stress the importance of hand washing.

Recipe for Hot Cross Buns (approximately twelve)

1 lb. flour	Pinch of salt
$\frac{3}{4}$ oz. yeast	2 oz. margarine
2 tablespoons caster sugar	2 oz. currants
1 level teaspoonful powdered cinnamon	1 egg
1 level teaspoonful mixed spice	About $\frac{1}{2}$ pint milk

Here is what your child can do with your guidance.

Sieve flour with salt and spices, rub in fat and add prepared currants. Cream the yeast with a little of the sugar, add a little warm milk and pour into centre of flour, sprinkle lightly over with flour and leave for ten minutes. Mix to a stiff dough with beaten egg, adding a little milk if required. Cover with a clean cloth, stand in a warm place until the mixture rises and doubles in size. Divide into portions, mould into small buns, mark with a cross, and leave on a greased and floured tin. Allow to rise until half as large again. Bake in a hot oven five to eight minutes. Melt a little sugar in one tablespoonful of milk, and brush over the buns.

Talk about the picture. Help your child to speak in whole sentences—to say, for example, 'We have a bag of flour', or 'Our bag isn't green'. Talk about the ingredients, let her or him weigh them out and read the scales. Point out their differing textures (give her or him a little taste, too) and always, always use the correct words.

Dressing-up   What better idea than to have a party with the buns so cleverly made? Children love to dress up, of course, in grown-up clothes, and could have a dressing-up box of clothes no longer needed. They become deeply involved in their new temporary characters, following the same pattern day after day, wearing a favourite adult garment and insisting on being called 'Mr.' or 'Mrs.' or 'Aunty'. Their play often includes imaginary companions, pets or articles—a dream world maybe, but in it they are inventive and resourceful.

Probably Mother and Father will be drawn into the pretence. They should, of course, play along with it, for in this way children prove and exercise their power of original thought, their main tool for learning and progress. At this age fact and fancy may be equally real to a child and it would be wise to be a little permissive about this. It is usually an indication of the struggle between the enormous world of reality surging in on them, and their own private world of fantasy to which they turn for relief and satisfaction. We *think* out our problems—children *play* them out.

Ask your child to tell you about the picture. Ask if the children are wearing children's clothes or grown-up clothes. Ask which of the three girls he or she likes best and why. What are they eating, and how many buns are on the table?

Picking flowers   Children love flowers for their shape, scent and colour, and like to pick flowers. Often, however, they merely succeed in pulling off the heads, and are left with the feeling of having spoiled something which should have been treated with care.

Teach them to slide their fingers from the flower-head down the stem and then to pinch at the base of the stem in order to break it.

Let them arrange the flowers by themselves: cut-down plastic containers make unbreakable vases, which children can fill, empty and carry around in safety. A few stones in the bottom of these containers will stop them toppling over.

Talk about the picture and be a good listener.

Paste and paper

A child can find many uses for an out-of-date wallpaper pattern book. He or she is fascinated by the many colours and colour combinations and is also intrigued by the patterns. By the age of four, children begin to appreciate how line and colour can be controlled, and the pleasing effect of pattern-making.

They will identify the repetition of colours and patterns, cut them out and make up their own spectacular shapes and pictures. Sticking with paste is never easy for children, but they are willing to learn the technique. Show them how to wipe off surplus paste on the edge of the container, and how to hold down the paper while they paste it. They are anxious to learn because they are becoming more ambitious, anxious to show you and each other that they *can* compete. A little discreet help may eventually spark off a great deal of individual enterprise.

The line of standing figures is made by folding paper concertina-wise, drawing and cutting so that parts of the folds are left intact, and then opening out. Try other figures and shapes.

Discuss the picture with your child.

Building up Wooden building bricks can last through the whole of childhood and surely are among the most rewarding of play materials. Interest in them will never pall because they need never become the same thing twice.

We can see the growth of imagination and dexterity, from the first attempts to place one brick upon another to the elaborate structures built by the three or four-year-old, representing the world around—flats, garages, houses, underpasses, fly-overs, their complexity limited only by the child's imagination.

The satisfying solidarity of the wood, the ease of construction, the adaptability to other toys such as model cars or animals, all these challenge creativity. A collapse just means that the bricks can be built into something new —unlike so much of the flimsy, mechanical gadgetry at present offered for sale and which some childish mishap immobilises for good.

Shown in the illustration are the H. G. Wells bricks sold by Paul and Marjorie Abbatt Limited, of 74 Wigmore Street, London, W.1.

Talk to your child about the picture and be a good listener. He will want to tell you what is being built and what sort of bricks are used—small, long, large, flat, etc. Ask what he himself would build.

Footmarks in the snow

A little enthusiasm from a grown-up will often kindle intense and lasting interest in situations which would otherwise pass unnoticed by a child.

For instance, these children are looking at patterns made by differing footmarks in the snow—hopping birds, walking birds, a dog, a cat, a bicycle tyre, a car tyre, or the size of the prints of their own wellingtons compared with Father's.

We ourselves take all this for granted, but to the child everything is a new discovery. Fresh knowledge and new words expand and stimulate a young mind eager for information on the world around.

Talk about the picture. Most four-year-olds will be able to think back to a time when it snowed. If so, ask what can they remember about it.

Simple printing Cut-potato printing is fascinating and so simple as to be well within the capabilities of this age group. Let your child wash the potato. The pattern-cutting needs a sharp knife, so this is a job for Mother. On the cut face of the half-potato, make your pattern, cutting the potato away for half an inch and leaving the design standing out. As a variation to crosses, stars, moons, etc., you could cut an imitation tyre mark, boot print, wheel shape, bird's claw or dog's paw—things the children could see in snow or mud.

Use saucers of powdered colour mixed with water and a little Polycel or flour as thickening. Show the child how to hold the saucer steady while dipping in the potato and wiping off the excess paint on the saucer edge, also how to hold down the paper while printing and lifting off the potato again—helpful little hints on technique. The novelty of repetitive designs soon has children completely engrossed. For the larger potato, cut notches in the top to make a handle.

Talk about the picture. Suggest to what use the sheets of patterned paper might be put when the children have finished them, perhaps to cover a book or box, a tin for string or as a paper basket. The finished pattern will make a decorative picture in itself. Do allow these to be hung on the walls. A child is encouraged to further effort by this acknowledgement. Praise is the greatest incentive that can be given to a child.

Home-made play scales

Simple home-made scales such as these provide endless instruction and diversion, and they are very easily made. You will need:

One wooden coat-hanger with metal hook removed.
One empty cardboard cylinder about 12″ – 15″ long.
Two identical empty plastic cartons.
Two equal pieces of string about 14″ long.
One three-inch nail (or a little longer than the width of the cylinder).
A five or six-inch circle of stout paper.
A gimlet.
Several weighty pebbles.
One hair-grip.
Sellotape.

Seal up one end of the cylinder with the circle of paper and 'Sellotape'. Cut two slots with a sharp knife in the other end, about 1″ wide by 2″ deep. Put the pebbles (or anything weighty) into the bottom of the cylinder so that it stands upright and steady. Push the nail through the top of the cylinder, at right angles to the slots and about 1″ from the top. With a gimlet make holes in both ends of the coat-hanger. Also make two holes near the top of each carton, and exactly opposite each other, for the string. Let the children hang the cartons onto the ends of the coat-hanger by the strings, helping them with the knots. Push the hair-grip down through the hole in the centre of the coat-hanger and open out to go over the nail, so that the hanger can move freely in the slots. Your child's home-made scales are now ready for use.

Using real tools

Nothing is more discouraging to a child than to have toys or tools which prevent him from achieving the competence at which he most certainly aims, young though he is. Toy tools so often fall into this category. It is therefore much more satisfactory to give a child the real tools for the job, although it means that he has to be supervised.

Hammers, nails, pincers, screw-drivers, saws, and gimlets are all tools which he can learn to use with care. Chisels are best omitted, as they are the tools most likely to cause accidents.

Do not overlook cardboard or balsa-wood as suitable materials for learning the technique of sawing or knocking in nails etc. Fairly easy success is necessary to the beginner. There is a great deal of household material which the child can effectively use to make models which should, of course, be the result of his own imagination and inventiveness, however unreal they may seem to us.

Ask your child if he can name the articles which the children have used in their models—lids, cotton reels, empty tins, egg cartons. What tools are they using and what have they made?

Play with a purpose

These children are getting a very real sense of importance and satisfaction from their play. They are actually practising road drill, and developing their alertness and judgement as well as their physical control over whatever they are riding or pushing.

They are using the traffic lights and beacons which they have made themselves from junk material. They probably had the help of an adult in laying out and chalking the 'roads' and placing the signs, but this will in no way detract from their pleasure.

Children nearing school age rely a great deal on the interest and encouragement which adults can give when helping to find the materials they need for their imaginative play.

Talk about the picture. Let your child tell you what the children are doing.

More about water-play As has been emphasised in previous books in this series, all children like to play with water, whether it be filling and emptying, pouring, squirting, watering the garden, washing down the yard or the car, etc. Let them wash the kitchen floor, the door, the kitchen furniture or utensils. These children are doing a careful wash and wipe of their own particular possessions.

It is in the handling of water that children find so much pleasure and relaxation and, by this age, growing control and dexterity are making it a much less messy business than at two or three.

Here is a little jingle, with actions:

If all the seas were ONE SEA
　　What a BIG SEA that would be.
If all the trees were ONE TREE
　　What a BIG TREE that would be.
If a man cut down the TREE
　　So that it fell into the SEA
What a BIG SPLASH THAT WOULD BE.

Talk about the children and the toys they are washing, the names of the parts, such as 'wheels', 'pedals', 'handlebars'. Ask what else might they wash afterwards.

Learning to sew

Card is the best material for the first sewing lesson: small hands find sewing on flimsy cloth so difficult that this skill is often needlessly left unmastered until school age.

Give a child some old greeting cards, a fairly big nail, a hammer, and an under-surface of thick card or a piece of wood to work on and let her, or him, first punch the holes.

Then, for sewing, a large bodkin is the obvious choice, with wool that has been threaded by Mother, doubled and knotted at the end. Over-sewing is the easiest stitch with which to start, the child putting the bodkin downwards through the holes and pulling it from underneath. Allow him, or her, to master and enjoy this accomplishment thoroughly before teaching any variation of stitch, the child's own pace of learning being the right one, of course.

A long piece of card with holes punched in pairs, together with a shoe lace, will provide practice in lacing and tying knots or bows. Also show them how to make a woollen ball:-

1. Thread the wool all around a cardboard ring several times.
2. Draw all strands together with a piece of wool threaded between card and strands. Tie tightly.
3. Cut wool around outer edge, draw up thread tightly and tie. Remove card.

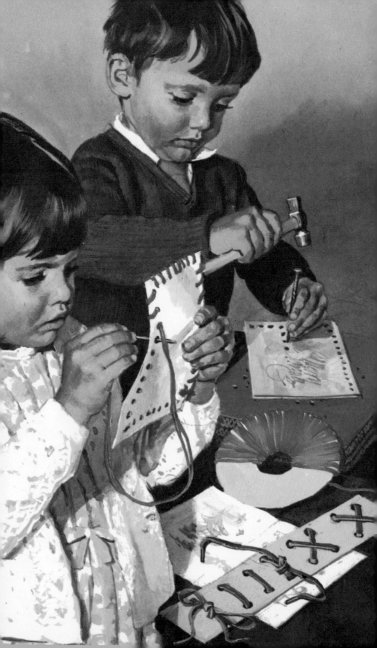

Sand-play   Children of four, boys in particular, are very interested in 'transport' toys that work.

It is true also that the toys they can work themselves, rather than the mechanically propelled ones, are best for them, being the most adaptable, giving the most pleasure and usually lasting the longest.

Here are children playing with sturdy wooden toys, using them with that most generally useful of all play material—sand. We need continually to remember that sand as play material justifies its use throughout all the childhood years, is always appropriate and varies only in the uses to which it is put.

The toys illustrated are made by Paul and Marjorie Abbatt Limited of 74 Wigmore Street, London, W.1.

Talk about the picture. If you have copies of 'Learning with Mother' Books 1, 2 and 3, your child can compare the sand-play pictures and talk to you about them. Always be a good listener.

Ask your child to find the page from which each picture is taken, and talk about what is happening there.